FIELD NOTES

~

For The Arrowhead Collector's
Recorded Discoveries

F. Scott Crawford

&

co-authored by:

_____

whose finds are documented herein.

ISBN: 1-46800-648-7
ISBN-13: 978-1468006483

DEDICATION

For Maggie, "forever and forever."

CONTENTS

FOREWORD

This is a special book!

Part of it is written with some ideas and hints for making records of your own personal discoveries of artifacts in the field. Such as arrowheads, scrapers, knives, drills, dart points and other ancient stone tools or pieces of pottery and other accoutrements of ancient lifeways which you may find.

Yet, most of this "Field Notes ~ For the Arrowhead Collector's Recorded Discoveries" book has not been written. It waits for your input. For your field notes. For your sketches. For your written tales of explorations and discoveries which have not yet taken place.

So, it is mostly your book. And the stories it captures are yours. Written to document your collection, for you, by you. In that way, the most important part of this book waits for you.

Take "Field Notes", sharp pencils or a pen and your camera along with you on your journeys of exploration. Write down the story of your finds. Make a sketch or two in the pages of your history book. Take some sharp "in-situ" photographs while your heart beats to the tempo of your discoveries.

As you create the text of "Field Notes ~ For The Arrowhead Collector's Recorded Discoveries" it will always be your own book of knowledge. Use as many copies of "Field Notes ~ For The Arrowhead Collector's Recorded Discoveries" as you need. This could be the first volume in your personal library of your own books about your personal and family collection of artifacts.

FSC

1 ~ WHY KEEP A RECORD AT ALL?

Why is it important to record and maintain information about the origin of the artifacts in a collection? Imagine how much more any collection could tell us if that data was known.

Recently the author acquired some of the artifacts from a collection which was put together in the 1950's and 1960's by a gentleman who lived in Ohio. His collection was sold by a relative to a Cincinnati area artifact dealer. In our correspondence about some of the ancient tools and weapons which I purchased, we discussed the possibility of obtaining any additional information about the original finders and the locations in which the pieces were discovered.

The answers which we shared had a great deal to do with the creation of this arrowhead collector's book: "Field Notes ~ For The Arrowhead Collector's Recorded Discoveries".

You see, the Ohio collector is now in a long term care facility and no longer able to provide any information to his family about these pieces. The data is now forever lost. When his family provided the assembled artifacts to the dealer, they gave all the information, which was available, to the dealer. However, that information was limited to a label on a few bags which contained the pieces: each bag was marked with the state from which the artifacts came.

Nothing more.

All additional information, which the collector may have known about the projectile points, knives, dart points, arrowheads or spear points in the different state-grouped bags, is no longer available.

The point I am trying to make is this: if you have a collection of artifacts, and knowledge of where the pieces were found, when they were found, by whom and under any particular circumstance, it is important to make a record of this information, so that in the future, others will also be able to have this vital data available, to better understand and appreciate the artifacts in your collection which has been gathered with such care and enthusiasm.

Otherwise, what your family will have is an assembly of interesting pieces, which have no history, no heritage, no provenance, and no scientific value.

There are several ways to record the information which will maintain the historic value of the pieces in your collection. Among them is keeping a notebook with collecting information, with identifying numbering and sketches of the artifacts. Many collectors write the important data on the less attractive side of the artifact, with permanent ink on the stone. And, today, many collectors make digital images of the artifacts, including vital information in the name of the file, etc., etc.

The main thing is to record the time period in which the artifact was found, the location, the finder, any special circumstances which may help to understand the event or make a record of any interesting story related to the discovery.

Then, make sure that this information is somehow permanently connected to your collection, so that the data does not inadvertently get discarded or misplaced.

2

2 ~ HOW TO USE "FIELD NOTES"

When you notice an artifact on the surface of ground which you are carefully inspecting, such as in a recently plowed field or along a fence line, and the artifact is something which you wish to document, you may want to first take a digital photograph of the piece as you first noticed it. This is what we call an "in-situ" photograph, made before you move the artifact. It is often useful to make additional photographs as you move the piece or turn it over.

Then, you make notes about the find. The date and location, with a description of the discovery site on the land, and any unusual or particular details which might be interesting to record.

Describe the artifact, with your idea of its intended use, physical condition of the piece, if it is whole or broken, worn, reworked, etc., information which can help understand the piece and the people who used it so long ago.

Describe the kind of material from which the relic is made. Is it flint, obsidian, quartz, agate, jasper, chert, bone, wood, pottery, or whatever it might be.

If you have an idea of the specific type of artifact, record that as a field identification. This can be subject to your future review of the technology or style of implement in additional resources.

Now, make a sketch or tracing of the artifact, both sides and other views as you like. This records the discovery and its condition.

3

EXAMPLE

Alkali
deposited
this side →

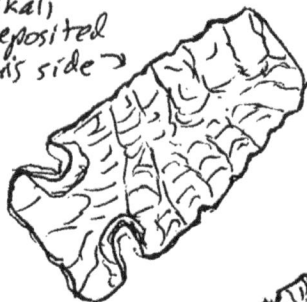

Clean,
exposed
surface

TRACE & SKETCH
by F. Scott Crawford 12/5/2011

Date: _1953 March_

Location: _Catlow Valley, Oregon_
N.E. of French Glenn, Oregon

Description: _Surface find, long undisturbed,_
one side is wind & dust polished. Tip
broken in use, base is complete.

Material: _Obsidian, Alkali one side_

Field Identification: _Northern SideNotch_
Dart Point

Signature: _found by Vernon Imel_

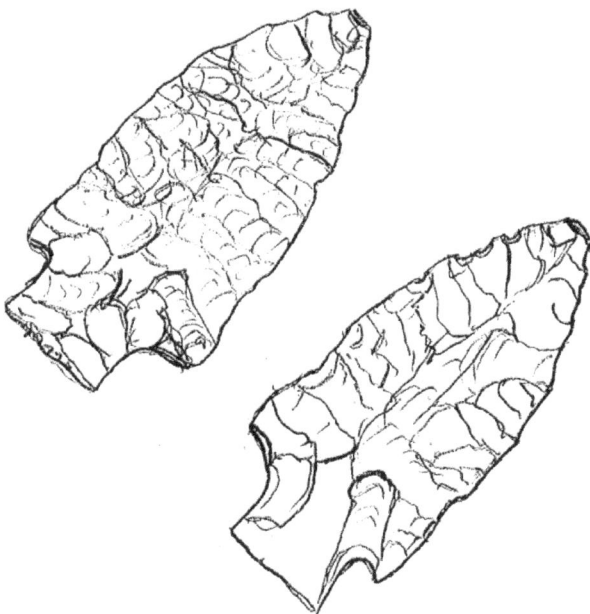

EXAMPLE

TRACE & SKETCH
by F. Scott Crawford 12/5/2011

Date: July 1966

Location: Logging Road of T. McElroy farm, West Fork of Brush Creek, 3 miles from Crawfordsville, Linn County, Oregon

Description: Large Jasper dart point, minor tip damage, one barb anciently broken, 3 small edge chips, knapping?

Material: Red Jasper

Field Identification: Scottsbluff dart point

Signature: FOUND BY [signature]

5

3 ~ "FIELD NOTES"

The artifacts documented in this "Field Notes" book cover explorations and discoveries from the following period of time:

_____ through _____.
(Month/Year)   (Month/Year)

Date:_____

Location:_____

_____

_____

Description:_____

_____

_____

Material:_____

Field Identification:_____

_____

Signature:_____

Date:_____

Location:_____

_____

_____

Description:_____

_____

_____

Material:_____

Field Identification:_____

_____

Signature:_____

Date:_____

Location:_____

_____

_____

Description:_____

_____

_____

Material:_____

Field Identification:_____

_____

Signature:_____

Date:_____

Location:_____

_____

_____

Description:_____

_____

_____

Material:_____

Field Identification:_____

_____

Signature:_____

Date:_____

Location:_____

_____

_____

Description:_____

_____

_____

Material:_____

Field Identification:_____

_____

Signature:_____

Date:_____

Location:_____

_____

_____

Description:_____

_____

_____

Material:_____

Field Identification:_____

_____

Signature:_____

Date:_____

Location:_____

_____

_____

Description:_____

_____

_____

Material:_____

Field Identification:_____

_____

Signature:_____

Date:_____

Location:_____

_____

_____

Description:_____

_____

_____

Material:_____

Field Identification:_____

_____

Signature:_____

Date:_____

Location:_____

_____

_____

Description:_____

_____

_____

Material:_____

Field Identification:_____

_____

Signature:_____

Date:_____

Location:_____

_____

_____

Description:_____

_____

_____

Material:_____

Field Identification:_____

_____

Signature:_____

Date:_____

Location:_____

_____

_____

Description:_____

_____

_____

Material:_____

Field Identification:_____

_____

Signature:_____

Date:_____

Location:_____

_____

_____

Description:_____

_____

_____

Material:_____

Field Identification:_____

_____

Signature:_____

Date:_____

Location:_____

_____

_____

Description:_____

_____

_____

Material:_____

Field Identification:_____

_____

Signature:_____

Date:_____

Location:_____

_____

_____

Description:_____

_____

_____

Material:_____

Field Identification:_____

_____

Signature:_____

Date:_____

Location:_____

_____

_____

Description:_____

_____

_____

Material:_____

Field Identification:_____

_____

Signature:_____

Date:_____

Location:_____

_____

_____

Description:_____

_____

_____

Material:_____

Field Identification:_____

_____

Signature:_____

Date:_____

Location:_____

_____

_____

Description:_____

_____

_____

Material:_____

Field Identification:_____

_____

Signature:_____

Date:_____

Location:_____

_____

_____

Description:_____

_____

_____

Material:_____

Field Identification:_____

_____

Signature:_____

Date:_____

Location:_____

_____

_____

Description:_____

_____

_____

Material:_____

Field Identification:_____

_____

Signature:_____

Date:_____

Location:_____

_____

_____

Description:_____

_____

_____

Material:_____

Field Identification:_____

_____

Signature:_____

Date:_____

Location:_____

_____

_____

Description:_____

_____

_____

Material:_____

Field Identification:_____

_____

Signature:_____

Date:_____

Location:_____

_____

_____

Description:_____

_____

_____

Material:_____

Field Identification:_____

_____

Signature:_____

Date:_____

Location:_____

_____

_____

Description:_____

_____

_____

Material:_____

Field Identification:_____

_____

Signature:_____

Date:_____

Location:_____

_____

_____

Description:_____

_____

_____

Material:_____

Field Identification:_____

_____

Signature:_____

Date:_____

Location:_____

_____

_____

Description:_____

_____

_____

Material:_____

Field Identification:_____

_____

Signature:_____

Date:_____

Location:_____

_____

_____

Description:_____

_____

_____

Material:_____

Field Identification:_____

_____

Signature:_____

Date:_____

Location:_____

_____

_____

Description:_____

_____

_____

Material:_____

Field Identification:_____

_____

Signature:_____

Date:_____

Location:_____

_____

_____

Description:_____

_____

_____

Material:_____

Field Identification:_____

_____

Signature:_____

Date:_____

Location:_____

_____

_____

Description:_____

_____

_____

Material:_____

Field Identification:_____

_____

Signature:_____

Date:_____

Location:_____

_____

_____

Description:_____

_____

_____

Material:_____

Field Identification:_____

_____

Signature:_____

Date:_____

Location:_____

_____

Description:_____

_____

Material:_____

Field Identification:_____

_____

Signature:_____

Date:_____

Location:_____

_____

_____

Description:_____

_____

_____

Material:_____

Field Identification:_____

_____

Signature:_____

Date:_____

Location:_____

_____

_____

Description:_____

_____

_____

Material:_____

Field Identification:_____

_____

Signature:_____

Date:_____

Location:_____

_____

_____

Description:_____

_____

_____

Material:_____

Field Identification:_____

_____

Signature:_____

Date:_____

Location:_____

_____

_____

Description:_____

_____

_____

Material:_____

Field Identification:_____

_____

Signature:_____

Date:_____

Location:_____

_____

_____

Description:_____

_____

_____

Material:_____

Field Identification:_____

_____

Signature:_____

Date:_____

Location:_____

_____

_____

Description:_____

_____

_____

Material:_____

Field Identification:_____

_____

Signature:_____

Date:_____

Location:_____

_____

_____

Description:_____

_____

_____

Material:_____

Field Identification:_____

_____

Signature:_____

Date:_____

Location:_____

_____

_____

Description:_____

_____

_____

Material:_____

Field Identification:_____

_____

Signature:_____

Date:_____

Location:_____

_____

_____

Description:_____

_____

_____

Material:_____

Field Identification:_____

_____

Signature:_____

Date:_____

Location:_____

_____

_____

Description:_____

_____

_____

Material:_____

Field Identification:_____

_____

Signature:_____

Date:_____

Location:_____

_____

_____

Description:_____

_____

_____

Material:_____

Field Identification:_____

_____

Signature:_____

Date:_____

Location:_____

_____

_____

Description:_____

_____

_____

Material:_____

Field Identification:_____

_____

Signature:_____

Date:_____

Location:_____

_____

_____

Description:_____

_____

_____

Material:_____

Field Identification:_____

_____

Signature:_____

Date:_____

Location:_____

_____

_____

Description:_____

_____

_____

Material:_____

Field Identification:_____

_____

Signature:_____

Date:_____

Location:_____

_____

_____

Description:_____

_____

_____

Material:_____

Field Identification:_____

_____

Signature:_____

Date:_____

Location:_____

_____

_____

Description:_____

_____

_____

Material:_____

Field Identification:_____

_____

Signature:_____

Date:_____

Location:_____

_____

_____

Description:_____

_____

_____

Material:_____

Field Identification:_____

_____

Signature:_____

Date:_____

Location:_____

_____

_____

Description:_____

_____

_____

Material:_____

Field Identification:_____

_____

Signature:_____

Date:_____

Location:_____

_____

_____

Description:_____

_____

_____

Material:_____

Field Identification:_____

_____

Signature:_____

Date:_____

Location:_____

_____

_____

Description:_____

_____

_____

Material:_____

Field Identification:_____

_____

Signature:_____

Date:_____

Location:_____

_____

_____

Description:_____

_____

_____

Material:_____

Field Identification:_____

_____

Signature:_____

Date:_____

Location:_____

_____

_____

Description:_____

_____

_____

Material:_____

Field Identification:_____

_____

Signature:_____

Date:_____

Location:_____

_____

_____

Description:_____

_____

_____

Material:_____

Field Identification:_____

_____

Signature:_____

Date:_____

Location:_____

_____

_____

Description:_____

_____

_____

Material:_____

Field Identification:_____

_____

Signature:_____

Date:_____

Location:_____

_____

_____

Description:_____

_____

_____

Material:_____

Field Identification:_____

_____

Signature:_____

Date:_____

Location:_____

_____

_____

Description:_____

_____

_____

Material:_____

Field Identification:_____

_____

Signature:_____

Date:_____

Location:_____

_____

_____

Description:_____

_____

_____

Material:_____

Field Identification:_____

_____

Signature:_____

Date:_____

Location:_____

_____

_____

Description:_____

_____

_____

Material:_____

Field Identification:_____

_____

Signature:_____

Date:_____

Location:_____

_____

_____

Description:_____

_____

_____

Material:_____

Field Identification:_____

_____

Signature:_____

Date:_____

Location:_____

_____

_____

Description:_____

_____

_____

Material:_____

Field Identification:_____

_____

Signature:_____

Date:_____

Location:_____

_____

_____

Description:_____

_____

_____

Material:_____

Field Identification:_____

_____

Signature:_____

Date:_____

Location:_____

_____

_____

Description:_____

_____

_____

Material:_____

Field Identification:_____

_____

Signature:_____

Date:_____

Location:_____

_____

_____

Description:_____

_____

_____

Material:_____

Field Identification:_____

_____

Signature:_____

Date:_____

Location:_____

_____

_____

Description:_____

_____

_____

Material:_____

Field Identification:_____

_____

Signature:_____

Date:_____

Location:_____

_____

_____

Description:_____

_____

_____

Material:_____

Field Identification:_____

_____

Signature:_____

Date:_____

Location:_____

_____

_____

Description:_____

_____

_____

Material:_____

Field Identification:_____

_____

Signature:_____

Date:_____

Location:_____

_____

_____

Description:_____

_____

_____

Material:_____

Field Identification:_____

_____

Signature:_____

Date:_____

Location:_____

_____

_____

Description:_____

_____

_____

Material:_____

Field Identification:_____

_____

Signature:_____

Date:_____

Location:_____

_____

_____

Description:_____

_____

_____

Material:_____

Field Identification:_____

_____

Signature:_____

Date:_____

Location:_____

_____

_____

Description:_____

_____

_____

Material:_____

Field Identification:_____

_____

Signature:_____

Date:_____

Location:_____

_____

_____

Description:_____

_____

_____

Material:_____

Field Identification:_____

_____

Signature:_____

Date:_____

Location:_____

_____

_____

Description:_____

_____

_____

Material:_____

Field Identification:_____

_____

Signature:_____

Date:_____

Location:_____

_____

Description:_____

_____

Material:_____

Field Identification:_____

Signature:_____

Date:_____

Location:_____

_____

_____

Description:_____

_____

_____

Material:_____

Field Identification:_____

_____

Signature:_____

Date:_____

Location:_____

_____

_____

Description:_____

_____

Material:_____

Field Identification:_____

_____

Signature:_____

Date:_____

Location:_____

_____

_____

Description:_____

_____

_____

Material:_____

Field Identification:_____

_____

Signature:_____

ABOUT THE AUTHOR

F. Scott Crawford has been an arrowhead collector since 1962, when he found his first small arrowhead on the family farm in western Oregon. In college, he was interested in archaeology and participated one summer at an extensive "dig" in Jerusalem, and toured numerous on-going archaeological projects across the region. Over the years he has found many artifacts during his explorations across North America. Since 2009, he has published the monthly e-magazine "ACOTW ~ Arrowhead Collecting On The Web". "ACOTW" is available from his web site: www.ArrowheadCollectingOnTheWeb.com at no charge, which is almost as good as free. As an accomplished flint and obsidian "knapper" of ancient style tools and hunting weapons, the author brings a unique set of skills to the understanding of those ancient artifacts which he enjoys collecting and about which he writes in the e-magazine. Scott and his wife, Maggie, live in Carrollton, Texas.

F. SCOTT CRAWFORD

Made in the USA
Monee, IL
10 December 2020